Canvas embroidery for beginners

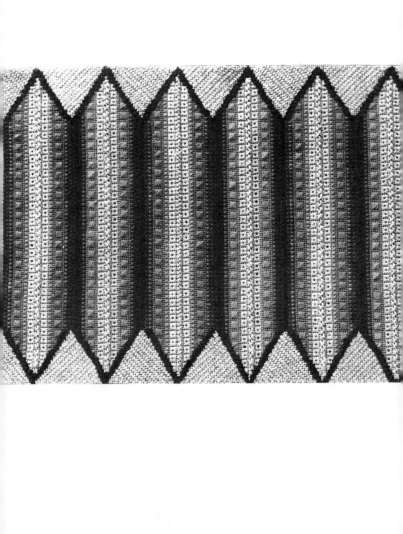

Canvas embroidery for beginners

Sylvia Green

Studio Vista
Watson-Guptill Publications New York

Acknowledgements

The author would like to thank all those people who so kindly lent their work to be photographed for this book; and to express appreciation to the Principal of Stockwell College of Education and Diana Springall for permission to photograph a student's work for fig. 87. She would like to thank the Embroiderers' Guild for permission to include examples of work from their portfolio collection.

Special thanks are due to John Gay, who took most of the photographs; to Mary Rhodes who supplied photographs of her own and her students' work for figs 6, 21, 26, 60, 82, 84, 85, 86, 88, 89, 90, 92, 100 and the title page; to Miss C. How and Mrs E. Maskell, who made and embroidered the bag for fig. 36; and to Phyllis Gibbon who typed the manuscript.

General Editors Brenda Herbert and Janey O'Riordan
© Sylvia Green 1970
Reprinted 1973
Published in London by Studio Vista
35, Red Lion Square, London WC1R 4SG
and in New York by Watson-Guptill Publications
1, Astor Plaza, New York, NY 10036
Library of Congress Catalog Card Number 79-99303
Set in 9 on 9½ pt Univers
Printed in the Netherlands
by Grafische Industrie Haarlem B.V.
ISBN 0 289 79699 7

Contents

Introduction

To many people who find pleasure and enjoyment in this kind of work, embroidery on canvas is associated with the repetitive use of one or two stitches only, usually worked in woollen thread (yarn) to cover completely the evenly-woven canvas ground, and reproduce in stitchery the picture or pattern already painted on it.

It comes as a surprise when they learn that there is a wide and interesting variety of canvas embroidery stitches, many of them decorative in themselves, and able to give rich, varied pattern and texture.

These stitches are not difficult to learn or to work, and it is fascinating to discover through a little practice how many simple and effective variations, and different ways of combining them, there are.

With this knowledge, and a willingness to experiment, it is not beyond the capabilities of anyone interested to invent attractive patterns and plan original designs. It is the purpose of this book to help them to do this, for there is infinitely more delight and satisfaction to be had from the simplest thing created through one's own thought and effort than from a more elaborate piece which demands no more than the monotonous embroidering of one stitch for its making.

Many of the photographs which illustrate this book are of experimental stitch samplers and finished work by people who were exploring the possibilities of this more creative approach for the first time. Indeed, for some of them, it was their first experience of any kind of canvas embroidery. All of them enjoyed what they did, and most of them were delightedly surprised to find in themselves an aptitude and inventiveness hitherto unrealized.

With the wide choice of threads and colours available today, canvas embroidery offers endless scope to the adventurous worker; a decorative wall-hanging may become a work of art in its own right; a finely-worked evening bag gain a value beyond mere perfection of stitchery, while cushions, chair seats and stool tops can be planned to suit the contemporary interior, which calls for simple uncomplicated shapes, clear colours and textural richness.

Fig 1   The simple shapes of this design are enriched with a variety of stitches including cross, upright cross, Smyrna, Florentine, reverse tent, and upright Gobelin (see also fig. 73, from which this is a detail)

Fig 2 (*over page*)   The Bradford Table Carpet, English, late sixteenth century. Embroidered with coloured silks, in tent stitch on linen canvas. Victoria and Albert Museum, London. Crown copyright

Inheritance from the past

The practice of enriching an evenly-woven fabric by embroidering stitches over the counted threads is an ancient and a universal one. Many of the stitches we now term 'canvas stitches' have in the past been used in a variety of ways on all kinds of material with an even weave. It is comparatively recently that they have become so exclusively associated with the special open-mesh canvases with which we are familiar.

A study of historical examples shows how methods and designs have changed through the centuries, according to the materials, the purpose of the work, and the social background. This helps us to understand that while we use the same stitches today, the different threads and materials at our disposal lead us to use them in a new way (figs 9 and 91). Any living art or craft must be constantly re-created, otherwise it ceases to have life.

The fourteenth-century burse in fig. 3 shows particularly well the typically geometric character of design on the counted thread. It is embroidered with silks in cross and plait stitch, which cover the whole surface of the fine hand-woven linen. The design, which has great clarity and simplicity, incorporates many Christian symbols and it quite plainly belongs to its time and to the great period of English ecclesiastical embroidery.

The famous Bradford Table Carpet (fig. 2), with its delightful pictorial border depicting scenes from Elizabethan country life, as plainly belongs to sixteenth-century England. It is embroidered with silks in tent stitch, which admirably 'draws' the details of the participants engaged in their lively pastoral pursuits and sports. The landscape includes the manor house and the mill, oak trees laden with acorns and flourishing fruit trees. The lord and lady of the manor stroll serenely among all the activity, and it is an enchanting and dignified record.

Colour was introduced into the wood-panelled rooms of the sixteenth-century home by the large wall-hangings which were embroidered in tent stitch in imitation of the costly and treasured medieval woven tapestries. Tent stitch worked on a fine linen canvas was found to be ideal for reproducing the character and detail of a woven tapestry. This seems to have led to some confusion about the distinction between embroidery on canvas, which is worked with a needle and thread onto a woven ground, and tapestry, which is woven on a warp; and no doubt accounts for the misnomer 'tapestry work' which is so often wrongly applied to canvas embroidery.

An increasing number of different stitches were used during the seventeenth century, and samplers of this time, worked with silk

Fig 3   Burse, English, 1290–1340. Embroidered with coloured silks in cross and plait stitch on linen. Victoria and Albert Museum, London. Crown copyright

and silver-gilt threads, record experiments made with stitches and combinations of stitches. Among these are Algerian eye or star stitch, Hungarian, Gobelin, Florentine, rococo (which was particularly popular), long armed cross and eyelet, as well as tent and cross stitch. Some of these samplers can be seen and studied in the Victoria and Albert Museum, London, and there is a particularly fine example in the Metropolitan Museum, New York, worked with silk and silver threads, which includes rococo, eyelet, Gobelin, tent and cross stitch.

The fashion for upholstering sets of chairs and matching settees became popular in the late seventeenth and early eighteenth centuries, and embroidery on canvas was used by the great furniture designers of the time. Chair seats and chair backs were covered with the most exquisite work in tent stitch and cross stitch. The stylized floral designs were worked in brilliantly-coloured wools (yarns) and silk threads, and it says much for the durability of the wools (yarns) and the suitability of tent and cross stitch for upholstery purposes, that so many chairs of this period can still be seen today in museums and private collections.

The nineteenth century has left us a much less welcome legacy. With the coming of machines and mass production, came too a

Fig 4 Sampler, English, mid seventeenth century. Embroidered with silk, silver and silver-gilt threads on linen, in a variety of stitches including tent, back, cross, plaited braid and rococo. Victoria and Albert Museum, London. Crown copyright

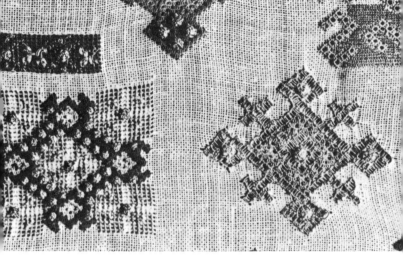

Fig 5   Detail from fig. 4

loss of artistic integrity and of taste. This is reflected in the immense popularity in England and America of the Berlin wool work pictures, the aftermath of which is with us to this day. Canvas was supplied with painted on 'designs' – of such subjects as little girls and pet dogs, parrots, stags, sprays of flowers and ivy – all ready for working in cross stitch with wools in colours of the utmost crudity and harshness, produced by the then new aniline dyes. Realism and a superficial cleverness were the qualities most admired and aimed for. The true craftsman's respect for his materials, which hitherto had resulted in individual work of such high quality, was all forgotten.

It is regrettable that work of so little intrinsic worth should have had such a wide and lasting influence, but now, in the second half of the twentieth century, canvas embroidery, in common with other kinds of embroidery, is enjoying a renaissance. A bold and imaginative use of the stitches, an eagerness to experiment with working them in new ways, with new threads, on all kinds of ground materials – from the conventional canvases to something as unconventional as aluminium gauze (metal wire mesh woven exactly like canvas) – is bringing a new vitality to a form of embroidery which had become stereotyped and lifeless.

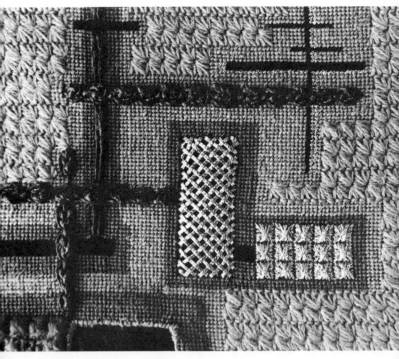

Fig 6   Detail from a panel by Jean Hayne. Surface stitches in creosoted string and gold threads have been used with the canvas stitches. This, and fig. 7, examples of contemporary canvas embroidery, illustrate the way in which the geometric nature of the canvas influences the design, and show the rich pattern and texture of the stitches.

Fig 7 (*opposite*)   Angel by G. Thackray

15

Materials

The choice of canvas

The texture of the fabric produced by your embroidery is decided as much by the coarseness or fineness of the canvas ground as by the threads and stitches which cover it, for to a great extent they will be chosen to suit the canvas ground. So it is essential that the canvas should suit the design and purpose of the work.

Selecting the right canvas from the wide range available today becomes second nature with experience, but to the inexperienced it may present a problem. It is helpful to know that there are two basic kinds of canvas: single-thread, which is woven with one thread warp (lengthwise), and one thread weft (widthwise) (fig. 8D) and Penelope or double-thread canvas, which has two threads warp and two threads weft (fig. 8B).

The single canvases are more pleasant to work on, and give best results, especially if a variety of threads and stitches are used. Double-thread canvas is more restricting, as it will not take some stitches, and beginners find the double thread confusing.

The more expensive linen canvases have better wearing qualities than the cheaper cotton canvases, and are recommended. Experienced workers usually choose a good single-thread linen canvas, especially for upholstery or for anything that will receive hard and constant wear. The canvas is fawn in colour and restful to the eye; the white canvases are inclined to dazzle and more easily show through the stitches.

The fineness or coarseness of the canvas is determined by the number of woven threads to the inch. Single canvas is available in a range varying from 10 to 32 threads to the inch. Most people will find one with 14 or 16 threads to the inch easy to work on; and this is suitable for such things as cushions, chair seats and hassocks as well as for purely decorative things, like samplers and wall panels. For work requiring more careful detail, such as small bags, belts and boxes, an 18-thread-to-the-inch canvas could be used.

Raffia or buff single canvas (fig. 8C), made with 10 threads to the inch, is an inexpensive cotton canvas which, as well as being suitable for coarse canvas embroidery, is excellent for practice work, stitch samplers and wall panels. Also, the larger holes give scope for experimenting with thicker and less usual threads, such as Perlita (3-ply mercerized-cotton embroidery thread with a shiny finish, about as thick as 2-ply rug yarn), synthetic raffia and chenille yarn.

For larger hangings, rug canvas, made with 3, 4, or 5 holes to the inch, worked with carpet wool, raffia and a variety of weaving threads can be used to give bold and exciting effects (fig. 8A).

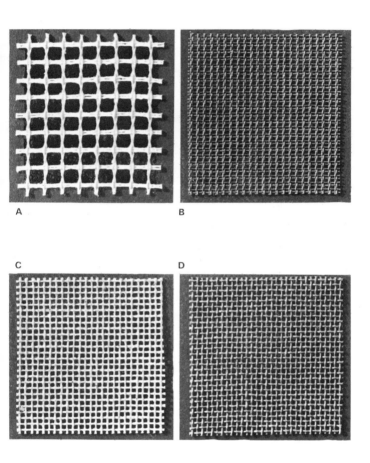

Fig 8   A rug canvas. B Penelope, double. C raffia canvas, single. 10 threads to 1 in.
D linen canvas, single. 12 threads to 1 in.

Fig 9 Embroidery with a variety of woollen threads on jute fabric. This detail, from the panel in fig. 91 by Diana Springall, shows an interesting and unusual use of threads and stitches

Jute embroidery fabric (fig. 9) is more closely woven than the other canvases. The thread is easy to see and to follow, and it is pleasant to work on. It can be used in exactly the same way as the other canvases – or for experimental or decorative work some of the ground can be left uncovered. The single open-mesh canvases are better for beginners, but it is good to experiment with different fabrics.

All these canvases can be bought in a variety of widths, and suppliers (see page 102 for names and addresses) will send detailed information or catalogues on request.

Threads

The choice of thread to be used for any work must depend directly upon the canvas selected and the purpose of the work. A large wall hanging will demand a coarser canvas, and therefore thicker threads, than a delicately-worked jewel box on a fine canvas, but each in its own way allows scope for an adventurous choice and use of thread. A hassock, on the other hand, will receive hard and constant wear, so there is a practical consideration as well. With these requirements in mind, it should be possible to choose wisely and appropriately from the great variety of conventional and unconventional threads at our disposal today. The basic threads for canvas embroidery are crewel wool (yarn) and tapestry wool, which are specially prepared to have hard-wearing qualities. Therefore, generally speaking, these are the best threads for making chair seats, cushions, kneelers (hassocks) and all things which have to stand up to constant use. Most are mothproofed.

Crewel wool (yarn), which is a fine 2-ply wool, is good for most purposes, a great point in its favour being that the number of strands threaded through the needle can be varied according to the stitch and the fineness or coarseness of the canvas used. When working with several strands, care should be taken to keep them from twisting, as this will make the stitches uneven.

Tapestry wool (yarn) is a thicker 4-ply wool, which is used as a single thread. Some people find this easier to manage, but it has the disadvantage of limiting the choice of canvas and stitches. If it is too thick, the stitches will push the mesh of the canvas out of shape and cause puckering, and on a coarser canvas it may not cover the mesh entirely. It tends to fluff up and wear thin in working if too long a thread is used; this makes the stitches uneven and affects the durability of the embroidered surface. There is no reason why both crewel and tapestry wools cannot be used on one piece of work, especially as they are made in a very wide range of identical colours and shades.

The use of other kinds of thread with the embroidery wools (yarns), where suitable, will add interest and variety to your work. Linen embroidery thread or weaving thread is as hard-wearing as the embroidery wools and gives excellent contrast. Stranded embroidery cotton (thread) and pearl cotton give a pleasant sheen against the woollen threads, but it must be remembered that these are less hard-wearing and should be used with discretion. With all these threads, which are made in lovely colours, the number of strands threaded in the needle can be varied according to the mesh of the canvas, as with crewel wool (yarn).

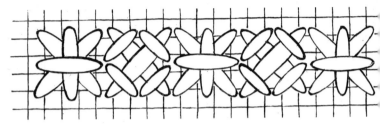

Fig 10   Alternate Smyrna and rice stitches make this simple border

For the coarser canvases 2-ply carpet wool (yarn) is the basic thread. It is tougher than the embroidery wools, and is made in regular ranges of good colours. Details may be had from the suppliers (see page 102). The cheapest way to buy this wool is in hanks of medium or long threads, called thrums. These are the ends cut from the loom when weaving is finished, so the colours are mixed and will vary each time. A good supply of thrums is always useful. Broken hanks, containing different shades of one colour, are a little more expensive; but with one or two of these and a few brighter colours selected from the regular range to add to your thrums, you will be well supplied. However, when a quantity of any one colour is needed, it is necessary to order all the wool at one time, as no maker will guarantee to match further orders exactly. Tapestry needles, size 16, are needed for threads of this thickness, and can be obtained from the wool makers or suppliers.

When the work will not be subject to a great deal of wear and tear, or the purpose is purely decorative, it is possible to be much more adventurous in the choice and use of threads.

Knitting wools (yarns) are made in all kinds of textures and weights; many of these, and yarns such as chenille, Lurex mixtures, and gold-fingering (an untarnishable, gold-coloured yarn), can be introduced most effectively. Cotton embroidery threads with a sheen, for example Perlita, and linen embroidery threads, can be used with woollen threads to give contrasting textural richness. Some of the thicker rug wools will unravel successfully and give a soft texture, in contrast to the rougher nature of the thrums.

Experiments can be made with every kind of thread, from silk, wool and metal, to string, raffia, and the linen thread of the canvas itself (see fig. 88); and it is fascinating to discover how the different threads can enhance each other, and give interest and vitality to the work.

Equipment

It is important to provide yourself with the proper equipment for making your work pleasant and satisfying, and the result as perfect as possible.

SCISSORS
Two pairs of good scissors are needed: a small pair of embroidery scissors with pointed ends for cutting the threads, and a stronger pair for cutting the canvas, and the paper shapes which may be used for designing.

NEEDLES
Needles with blunt ends are used for working on canvas. These are called tapestry needles and can be bought in a variety of sizes, the most useful being from 18 to 21. However, the needle must always be selected carefully to suit the thread and the size of the canvas. A finer thread and canvas will require size 24 or 26, and a coarser thread and canvas size 13 or 14. The eye of the needle should be large enough to take the thread easily, and thread and needle should pass through the canvas mesh freely without pushing it out of shape.

THIMBLE
A thimble will prevent sore fingers and help work the stitches rhythmically and evenly.

PAIR OF TWEEZERS
When unpicking any embroidery, the stitches should be cut and the thread removed in short ends. A pair of tweezers is invaluable for plucking out these ends.

TAPE MEASURE
A tape measure is in constant use; for preparing the canvas and the design, for checking that it is not being pulled in working, and that the measurements of the finished work are accurate. A steel measuring tape is the most satisfactory and easy to use.

GRAPH PAPER
Graph paper with 8 or 10 squares to the inch is excellent for working out patterns and planning designs, as each square of the paper approximates to one stitch worked over two threads of the canvas. Tracing paper or its equivalent is also useful for designing.

TAPE
When the work is to be put on a frame, a supply of tape (about 6 yds) in $\frac{1}{2}$-in. and 1-in. width (bias tape in US) will be needed.

The embroidery frame

It is advisable to use an embroidery frame for any piece of work larger than about twelve inches, and for all fine work, especially if metal threads are introduced. It helps to ensure that the canvas keeps in shape and does not pucker (so long as the threads and stitches have been chosen appropriately), and that the stitches are worked evenly. This is a great advantage when making up the article, and assists in giving a rewardingly crisp finish to the work.

A square, or rectangular embroidery frame is a simple piece of equipment. It consists of two rollers with webbing firmly attached and slots at either end through which the two arms are fitted. These arms have holes at regular intervals into which the split pins, or screws, are placed to fix the four sides of the frame firmly in position. Framing-up, or dressing the frame as it is called, is a simple process, so if you have had no experience of this, do not let that deter you. The size of the frame is determined by the measurement of the webbing on the rollers. Frames can be bought (or made by a handyman) in various sizes.

A 26-inch frame is a useful size, and easy to manage. A round tambour frame is unsuitable for this kind of embroidery, as it pulls the canvas out of shape.

Preparing the canvas

Instructions are given for framing-up a piece of canvas measuring 19 in. × 24 in. on a 24-in. or 26-in. frame. This is the size recommended for working your first projects, a display sampler, and a cushion cover similar to the one illustrated on page 70. These two examples are worked on a single-linen canvas with 14 threads to the inch.

When cutting the canvas, it is important to remember that it must always be used with the selvedge (the edge, parallel to the warp) vertical, that is, on either side, not at the top and bottom, of the work. Never work the wrong way of the canvas; most canvases have a few more threads one way than the other, and this not only affects the look of the stitches but causes more serious difficulties if edges have to be matched when making up an article.

1 Cut the canvas 19 in. (high) × 24 in. (wide).
2 Mark the top of the canvas with a coloured stitch to distinguish it, and cut off the selvedge from the sides.
3 Tack (baste) a line through the centre of the canvas vertically and horizontally; use a fine cotton thread or one strand of crewel wool (yarn).

4 At the top and bottom edges fold down $\frac{1}{2}$-in. turnings and tack (baste), on the wrong side.
5 Turn and tack the two side edges in the same way, and then bind these with 1-in. wide tape or webbing (strong, closely woven, narrow fabric used for binding, reinforcement etc.). The tape can be pinned and tacked in place and then machine stitched, or sewn by hand with a double running stitch or a back stitch in strong cotton (thread).
The canvas is now ready for framing up.

Framing-up the canvas

1 Mark the exact centre of the webbing on the two rollers permanently.
2 Place the centre of the top edge of the canvas to the centre of the webbing, with the right side of the canvas to the right side of

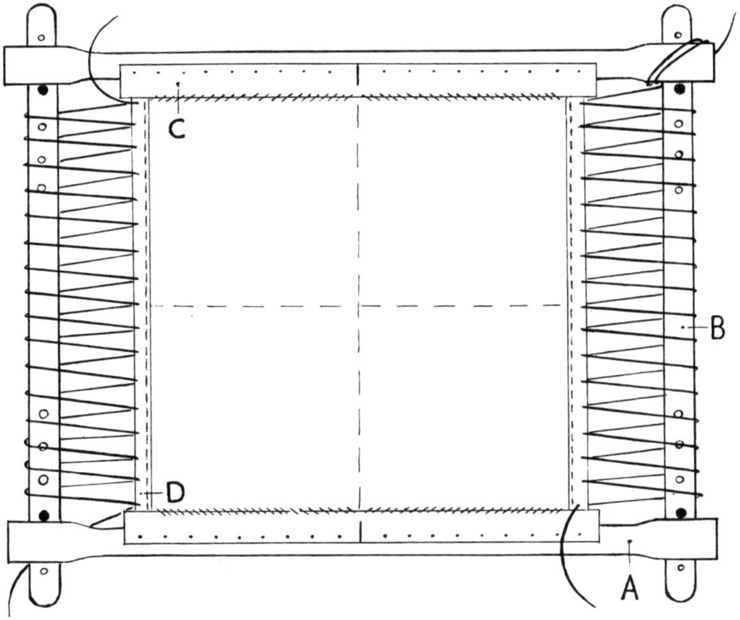

Fig 11   An embroidery frame: A roller B arm C webbing D tape

the webbing. Pin in position, with the pins at right angles to the edge, working from the centre first to one side and then the other. Tack (baste), and remove pins. With a strong thread, such as buttonhole twist, overcast the edges, starting at the centre and working to each side. Repeat this for the second roller.

3 You can now put the two arms of the frame in position by slipping the ends through the slots in the rollers. Extend the frame so that the canvas is taut, but not pulled too tight, and fix the four sides of the frame in place by putting the split pins or screws into the appropriate holes.

4 Lace the two sides of the canvas to the arms in either of the following ways: thread up a packing needle (a very large needle) with strong string or carpet thread. The length needed will be about 3 yds. Working from the centre to each side, take this through the taped edge and around the arm of the frame at intervals of about 1 in. Allow about 18 in. at either end for securing to the frame. Extend the frame so that the canvas is pulled tight and lace the sides firmly, securing the ends.

Or, begin by fully extending the frame, and tightening the canvas. Then take about 3 yds of $\frac{1}{2}$-in. wide tape. Fold in half and pin the fold in place at the centre of the taped edge of the canvas. Work from here to each side, taking the tape around the arm and pinning it to the canvas at intervals of $1\frac{1}{2}$ in. Secure the ends to the frame.

To keep the canvas taut as you work, it will be necessary to tighten the string, or the tape, from time to time. It is worth taking trouble to maintain an even tension, as this will keep your work in good shape and help in making the stitches regular.

Fig 12   This counter-change pattern could be used for an embroidered border, or to make an all-over pattern

The canvas for your first project is now framed-up and ready. On page 53 you will find suggestions about how to proceed.

Footnote The instructions given are for framing-up a relatively small piece of canvas, which is within the over-all measurements of the frame. The measurement of the canvas to be attached to the rollers can never exceed that of the webbing, but the length of canvas between the rollers can be considerably more than the length of the arms of the frame if necessary. For example, the canvas for an upright panel measuring 20 in.×30 in. could be worked on this size of frame by attaching the top and bottom edges to the rollers and winding the 30-in. length onto one of the rollers until the appropriate amount is left for lacing to the sides of the frame. As the work proceeds, the part which is embroidered is wound on to the top roller and more canvas released from the bottom roller until the work is complete. In the case of a long seat cushion of the same measurements, the edges attached to the rollers are the sides of the cushion. The frame is then turned for working, so that the rollers are on the right and left of the work, not at the top and the bottom; otherwise you would be working the wrong way of the canvas, as the selvedge sides are on the rollers this time (see fig. 11). When rolling finished embroidery around the roller, it is advisable to protect it by rolling in a sheet of tissue paper or soft fabric with it, but be very careful to keep this flat and uncreased. Once you have a piece of canvas framed up at the right tension, do not unlace and roll up until the embroidery on that area is complete if you can avoid it.

The stitches

The embroiderer delights in stitches in the same way as the writer delights in words. To each a good vocabulary is invaluable, and as a writer must learn to use words in a way that will not distort their true meaning, and yet express the thought or idea in his mind, so the embroiderer needs to gain understanding of the stitches and their proper use.

There are a great many canvas stitches, and while it is an advantage to know how to work as many as possible, it is not good to use too many different ones in a single piece of work. We shall learn more about this as we go along.

The stitches illustrated in this chapter are all basic and simple, but they are some of the most useful and decorative. A thorough knowledge and understanding of these will provide a good jumping-off ground for learning to use more elaborate stitches, as experience and confidence is gained.

Tent stitch is the best known and most popular canvas embroidery stitch; it gives a smooth, hard-wearing surface and is excellent for detailed work. It is worked across the intersection of one warp and one weft thread (fig. 28, page 38).

Cross stitch is a development of tent stitch (fig. 15, page 29). These two extremely simple stitches form the basis of a great many canvas embroidery stitches of rich, varied pattern and texture.

Before beginning to plan a piece of work, such as the attractive sampler on page 52, it will be necessary for the beginner to practise the stitches on a piece of canvas of the same kind as that to be used for the finished article. This practice sampler may turn out to be decorative in itself, but its chief purpose is for finding out how to work the stitches and experimenting with the various threads, and it should be approached in a free and adventurous spirit.

Try working the same stitch in different kinds of thread, and see how the surface texture can be varied without changing the stitch. Similarly, change the colour but not the stitch, or use different tones of one colour only. All these ways of working will give contrast without destroying harmony.

Those stitches which are decorative in themselves, such as rice stitch and double cross stitch, can be worked in a variety of ways to make delightfully-patterned areas, and some of the many ways of arranging and combining the stitches will be discovered on your first practice piece.

At the same time, much will be learned about the helpfulness, and the limitations, of the canvas ground. All this will contribute to your understanding of how to use the stitches to make simple

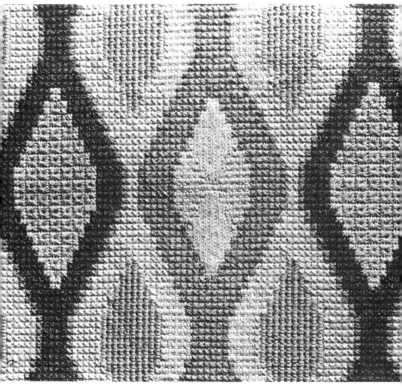

Fig 13   Detail from the stool top shown in fig. 76 by Norah Gibbon

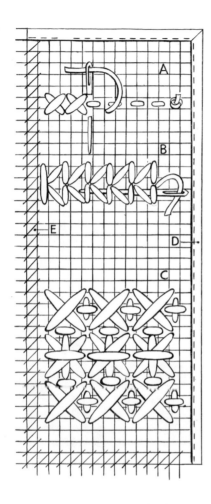

Fig 14

A beginning a stitch
(right side of canvas)

B finishing a thread
(wrong side of work)

C a border made with Smyrna
cross, large cross and straight
cross, and back stitch

D tape

E oversewn edge

patterns and plan satisfying designs, which is the aim of this book.

Fig. 14 shows how to begin working a stitch (A). Tie a knot in the end of the thread and take the needle through the canvas from the right side about 1 in. from the position of the first stitch. Darn the thread through the mesh, leaving the knot on the surface. As you work the stitches the thread is secured and covered, and the knot can be cut off. To finish off a thread, darn it into the back of the work for about $1\frac{1}{2}$ in. (B).

Crossed stitches

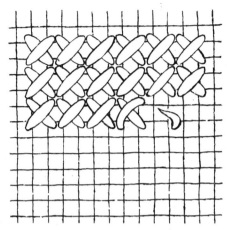

Fig 15.

Begin with the crossed stitches; most of them can be worked easily and quickly, and it is fascinating to discover the many ways in which they can be used and combined. All the stitches in this group are worked over 2 threads, or a multiple of 2 threads, of the canvas. They all use either the diagonal direction \ and / making × or the vertical and the horizontal making +, or are made up of a combination of all, or some, of these directions. They are all worked horizontally, from left to right and from right to left of the canvas.

A piece of canvas about 12 in. × 6 in. will make a good practice sampler. It should be cut with the selvedge vertical. The canvas will fray with handling. In order to prevent this, oversew the edges, or, if the sampler is to be used frequently for reference, bind them with tape. Limit your colours to three on this first piece, and let them be well contrasted in tone; for example, off-white, yellow ochre and coffee brown. A disciplined and considered use of colour and tone will allow you to show the full effectiveness of the pattern and texture of the stitches.

Cross stitch

Cross stitch is made by working across 2 threads of the canvas, diagonally from bottom right to top left, and then from bottom left to top right to complete one stitch (fig. 15). By working each stitch separately, the back of the canvas is well covered, and this makes a firm and hard-wearing fabric, which is an advantage. If the first arm of the cross is worked in a row from left to right and then the second arm from right to left, this does not cover the canvas so closely or give so firm a stitch.

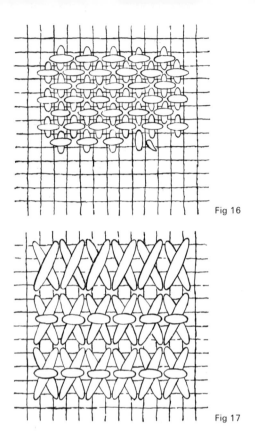

Fig 16

Fig 17

Straight or upright cross stitch

A vertical stitch over 2 threads of the canvas is crossed horizontally over 2 threads (fig. 16). Each row of stitches interlocks closely with the preceding row, and each stitch should be completed separately. It makes a close, firm, and pleasantly-textured surface.

Oblong cross stitch

This is worked from bottom right upwards over 4 horizontal threads and across 2 vertical threads, to top left; the stitch is completed from bottom left to top right (fig. 17).

It can be varied by working a back stitch over 2 threads at the middle of the cross. If it is in the same colour, the two stages should be completed before going on to the next stitch. It may also be worked separately in a different colour.

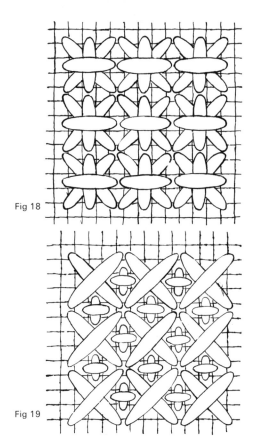

Fig 18

Fig 19

Double cross or Smyrna cross

A diagonal cross stitch worked over 4 threads each way of the canvas (see above) forms the basis of this and the next attractive stitch. Complete the diagonal cross first, then work the vertical of the straight cross, and finally the horizontal (fig. 18). This stitch can be worked in one colour, or two colours can be used to make a number of effective variations including a chequer pattern (see fig. 50). Experiments may also be made with the use of more than one kind of thread.

Large cross and straight cross

The large cross is worked first over 4 threads each way of the canvas, and then the small straight cross, which is fitted into the spaces between them over 2 threads each way of the canvas (fig. 19). Contrasting colours and threads will give interest.

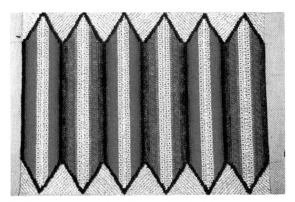

Fig 21   Embroidery for lamp base by Dorothy Falconer

Fig 22   Embroidered panel by Marjorie Bartlett

Fig 20 (*opposite*)   Cross stitch, straight or upright cross, large cross and straight cross, and Smyrna cross are among the stitches used in this example

33

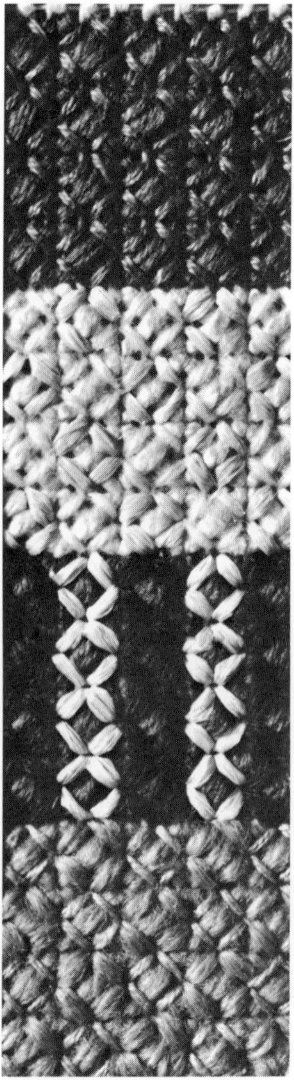

Fig 23 Rice stitch worked in a variety of threads.
A tapestry wool (yarn) and linen weaving thread
B the large crosses are worked in cream Perlita (shiny cotton embroidery thread). The diagonal stitches are worked to make alternate diamonds with white tapestry wool (yarn) and natural raffene (synthetic raffia).
C the large crosses are worked in light blue tapestry wool (yarn). The diamonds are worked in alternate vertical rows with dark blue wool and natural raffene.
D the large crosses are worked in a thread unravelled from a soft rug wool (yarn). The diagonal stitches are worked to make alternate diamonds with the same wool and a linen weaving thread

Fig 24

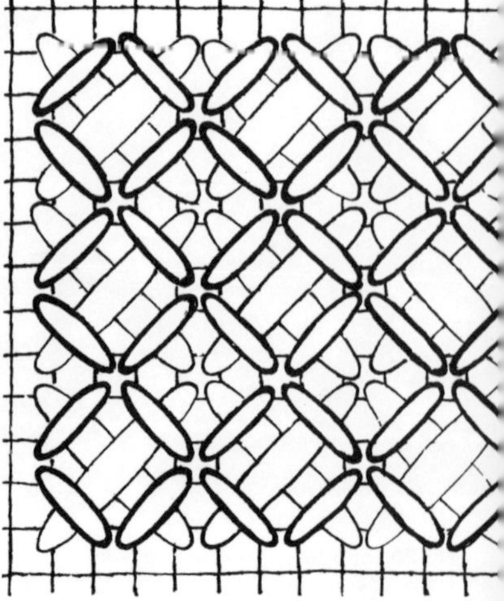

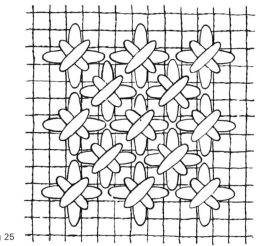

Fig 25

Double straight cross

This stitch makes a lovely knobbly texture and can be used in a number of interesting ways. A straight cross worked over 4 threads of the canvas is held down by a diagonal cross worked over 2 threads (fig. 25). It can be worked in one colour or two colours, in the same thread or contrasting threads; it can be chequered; it can be used to give a gradated effect, if the straight cross is worked in one colour, and the diagonal cross in bands of brighter and deeper tones of the same or a similar colour (see fig. 7).

Rice stitch

The cross stitch over 4 threads of the canvas is worked first, usually in a thick wool (yarn) or embroidery thread. A finer, contrasting thread, such as pearl cotton, cotton embroidery thread, or linen (thread), can be used for the small diagonal stitches, which are worked over 2 threads, each way of the canvas, so that they also form a cross. This is another composite stitch, which can be varied in a number of ways (see fig. 24).

Flat stitches

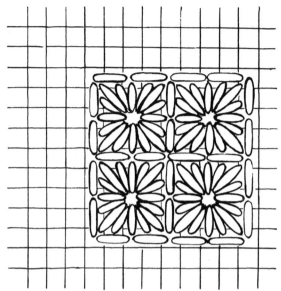

Fig 27
Eyelet stitch, worked in the same way as star stitch (fig. 38) but with 16 stitches instead of 8

Fig 26 (*opposite*)   Detail of stitches from the panel by May Thurgood illustrated in fig. 92 showing an appropriate and unusual use of tent stitch with cross stitch and eyelet stitch

Some of the stitches in this group can be recognized as a simple development from tent stitch. These all use the diagonal direction / or \. Others use straight stitches in a variety of ways, and two use all four ways of the canvas. Being flat, most of them offer the maximum scope for an imaginative use of threads to give textural contrast and interest, and some can be arranged to make delightful chequer or geometric patterns.

The illustration on the opposite page shows a very interesting and effective use of tent stitch as a contrastingly smooth background to cross stitch and eyelet, and for making a linear pattern. These are appropriate uses for this stitch, which is seen at its best when used in this way. It can appear rather dull and uninteresting when worked over large areas of background in unbroken colour. Petit Point is simply another name for tent stitch worked on a fine canvas in silk thread, or some other fine thread, and Gros Point is tent stitch worked in a thicker thread on a coarser canvas.

For an exciting and more experimental use of tent stitch see fig. 91.

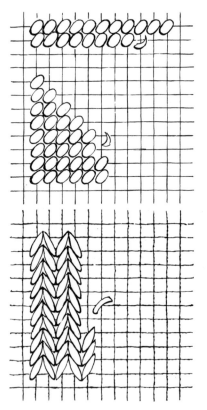

Fig 28

Fig 29

Tent stitch

Tent stitch is worked diagonally across the intersection of 1 warp and 1 weft thread of the canvas. The diagram (fig. 28) shows how to work it in horizontal rows, from right to left, and left to right across the canvas. When covering a large area with this stitch, it is usually better to work it in diagonal rows on the canvas (see fig. 28). This makes a more closely-knit, stronger fabric, and will more easily give an even surface. It makes an almost indestructible fabric, and can be worked in most threads.

Reverse tent stitch

The diagonal stitches are worked in vertical lines up and down the canvas, so that the diagonal directions alternate (fig. 29). Each stitch is worked over 1 vertical and across 2 horizontal threads. The size of the stitch can be varied by working over more threads – for example, over 2 vertical and 3 horizontal, and so on, according to the size required, or the coarseness of canvas and thread.

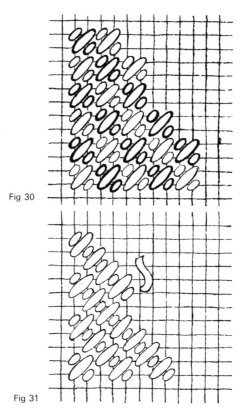

Fig 30

Fig 31

Some of the ways in which this stitch can be used are shown in fig. 33, and with a little practice you can discover others for yourself.

Mosaic stitch

The diagram shows clearly how mosaic stitch is worked in rows diagonally over 1, 2, 1, threads of the canvas (fig. 30). It can be worked in two colours, or white and one colour, and is most effective worked in wool (yarn) and silk threads. It is better to work the rows separately; first in one colour and thread, and then in the other.

Diagonal Florentine stitch

This is worked in diagonal rows, alternately over 1 and 2 threads of the canvas (fig. 31). The long stitches in each succeeding row fit in between the long stitches in the preceding row.

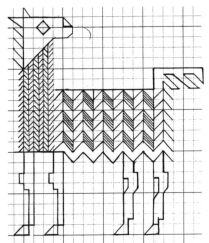

Fig 32 A sketch suggesting how the stitches in fig. 33 could be used

Fig 33 Reverse tent stitch. Top, worked with alternate dark and light wool (yarn). Bottom, worked in alternate rows of wool and coton à broder (unstranded embroidery cotton)

Fig 34 (*opposite*) Cock by Barbara Hudson, detail from fig. 93, showing tent stitch, reverse tent stitch, diagonal Florentine, straight cross and Smyrna cross

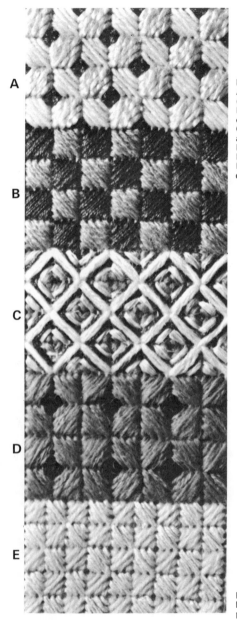

Fig 35   Flat stitch
A Perlita, and tapestry wool
(yarn)
B tapestry wool and linen
embroidery thread
C tapestry wool, linen thread,
and synthetic raffia
D unravelled rug wool and
Perlita
E tapestry wool and linen
embroidery thread

Fig 36 (*opposite*)   Flat stitch
has been used to embroider the
panel on this attractive bag

43

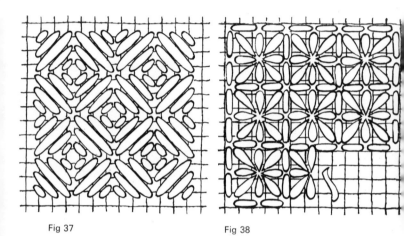

Fig 37   Fig 38

Flat stitch

Flat stitch is a form of mosaic stitch. It is worked in rows diagonally over 1, 2, 3, 2, 1, threads of the canvas, each row in the opposite direction to the previous one (fig. 37). It is well worth taking time to discover some of the attractive ways in which this most rewarding stitch can be used. The different directions of the stitches can be exploited to the full by working the rows alternately in tapestry wool (yarn) and silk or linen embroidery thread. Try this all in white; the effect is lovely. Threads, and colours too, can be arranged to make a variety of patterns (see fig. 35).

Star stitch or Algerian eye stitch

This is worked with 8 stitches, each one passing over 2 threads of the canvas (fig. 38). Begin with the upright stitch at top, work in a clockwise direction. The needle should always be taken down through the centre hole. If the canvas is not completely covered, a back stitch over 2 threads may be worked around each star stitch, preferably in the same colour. It makes an attractively-textured surface worked in one colour over an area. It can be used to give a chequered pattern, and in other ways, although it should be remembered that any stitch which is decorative in itself is usually

44

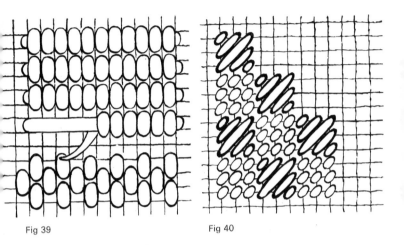

Fig 39   Fig 40

sufficiently effective without too much variation of colour, thread, or arrangement. Some practice is required in working this stitch with an even tension; it is very easy to pull the upright and horizontal stitches too tight.

Upright Gobelin

The straight stitches are worked over 2 threads in horizontal rows (fig. 39). It is usually an advantage to lay a thread along the canvas first, and work over it; this helps to give a pleasantly ribbed effect. It is a good background stitch, as it covers the canvas very thoroughly and is comparatively quick and easy to work. This is the stitch which most closely imitates the character of the woven tapestry, from which it takes its name. A variation of this stitch is shown in the lower half of the diagram.

Chequer stitch

This is a combination of diagonal stitch (a form of flat stitch) and tent stitch. The diagonal stitch is worked first in rows over 1, 2, 3, 2, 1, threads of the canvas; the remaining squares are then worked in tent stitch (fig. 40). It looks best worked all in the same colour and thread, as the two stitches vary the tone and texture sufficiently to make it interesting. For a smaller chequer stitch, work the diagonal stitch over 1, 2, 1, threads of the canvas.

Fig 41   Detail from cushion by Mary Hall in fig. 72. This lovely pattern of stitch and texture includes reverse tent, star stitch, upright Gobelin and variation, Parisian, tent, and flat stitch

Fig 42 (*opposite*)   Detail of fig. 98 showing upright Gobelin and variation and star stitch

46

47

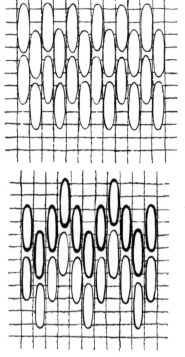

Fig 43

Fig 44

Bricking stitch

The upright stitches are worked over 4 threads of the canvas leaving 2 warp threads between each. The second and every succeeding row begins 2 threads lower, and the stitches fit closely between each other to make the bricking arrangement from which the stitch is named (fig. 43).

Florentine stitch

This stitch is so named because it originated in Florence. The upright stitches are worked over an even number of threads, usually 4 or 6, and each stitch is 'stepped' up or down 2 threads of the canvas to make the characteristic zig-zag pattern (fig. 44). It is a useful background stitch, and when covering large areas is usually worked in two or more rows of different colours, making an all-over wave pattern. Florentine, Flame, or Bargello work, as it is variously called, can fill a book on its own; its possibilities are endless. When it is introduced among other canvas stitches, it should be used with extreme simplicity and discrimination; it

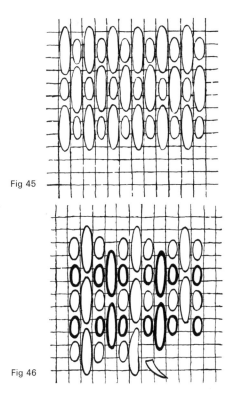

Fig 45

Fig 46

can easily appear too dominant and will immediately look out of place if wrongly used.

Parisian stitch

The upright stitches can be worked alternately over 1 and 3, or 2 and 4, threads of the canvas. The long stitches are worked below the short ones in each row (fig. 45). This stitch can be worked in two colours, or in one only, and is effective when threads of different thickness and texture are used.

Hungarian stitch

The straight stitches are worked from left to right in units of 3, over 2, 4 and 2 threads of the canvas, leaving 2 vertical threads between each unit. In the second row, the units are worked from right to left, into the same holes of the canvas, with the small stitches under the small stitches of the first row, and the long stitches between them (fig. 46). Hungarian stitch can be worked all in one colour, in contrasting colours or tones of one colour, and in contrasting threads of one colour, or of white.

Working the stitches

It is one thing to learn how a stitch is made, and another to work it evenly and well over an area of canvas. Tension is an important factor in working any embroidery stitch; it is especially so with canvas embroidery, for the stitches are making a fabric. Correct tension and even working depend to a large extent upon the right choice of thread for each of the different stitches. For example, on your practice sampler you will discover how a small close stitch like tent stitch requires a finer thread than a larger, looser stitch like double cross. The length of thread too must be considered. Too long a thread will prevent your pulling it through in one movement, and will cause additional unevenness because it will wear thin with being constantly passed through the rough canvas; a working thread of about 15 or 16 in. is suitable.

Once you are familiar with the stitches, practice will enable you to work them with increasing speed; the more quickly and rhythmically you work the more even they will be. The greatest of all aids to regular and smooth working is the embroidery frame, for this keeps the canvas itself at an even tension; it also allows both hands to be free for working, the needle passing easily from the right hand, on top, to the left hand, underneath the canvas, and back again. Be sure that the top stitches always slope or lie in the same direction, any deviation or irregularity will show at once, and will spoil the texture. Another good rule is to work every stitch in exactly the same order, so that they look alike on the back too, although not necessarily just like the front. Finally, as all the holes in the canvas will be worked into at least twice and sometimes as many as four times, whenever possible take the needle up through the free holes and down through the holes already worked into; this will disturb the stitchery as little as possible.

Instructions for beginning to work the stitches and finishing off the thread are given on page 28.

Fig 47 (*opposite*)   Bricking and Hungarian stitch worked on a background of long and short stitches arranged in bands

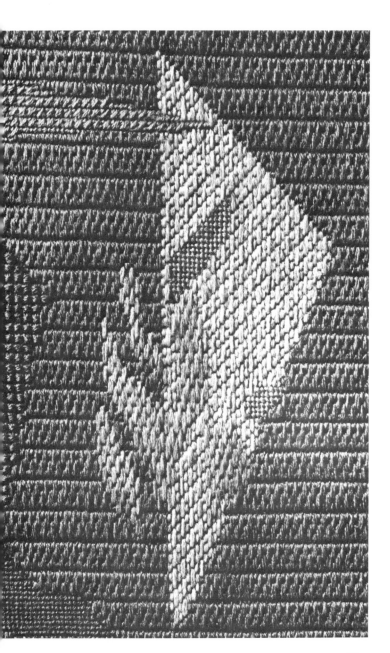

Your first project, a sampler

On your first practice sampler you will have found out how to work a number of stitches, and discovered something about their decorative and textural qualities. The folder sampler on page 52 is designed to give practice in working a selection of stitches and in using and combining some of them to embroider a simple, well-balanced motif. In working such a sampler you will be taking a first step towards designing with the stitches and creating a truly personal piece of work.

The left-hand panel provides twelve units, each $1\frac{1}{2}$ in. square, for working the stitch sampler; the right-hand panel is for the motif. Crewel wool (yarn) is suggested for working both panels, in order that you may gain experience in suiting the thickness of thread to the various stitches. It is suggested that the following stitches are included among the twelve selected: rice stitch, Smyrna stitch, star stitch, flat stitch, Hungarian stitch, and bricking stitch.

Colour is a most important factor, and with this first piece you should practise and demonstrate a purposeful choice and use of colour. Limit your colours to three which are well contrasted in tone. Some of the more decorative and composite stitches depend more upon contrast of tone for their effect than upon actual colour, and the excellent sampler on page 52 shows very well the satisfying unity and balance which can be achieved with limited colour carefully chosen, and a considered use of tone.

To fulfil its purpose any sampler must aim at being as perfectly worked and made as possible; in however small a way it is a work of reference as well as a delightful thing to make and to look at. For this, if for no other reason, a canvas embroidery sampler should be worked on a frame. Instructions for framing up a piece of canvas of the size required for making this sampler have been given on page 23.

Your finished work will be enhanced by the mounting (matting) and it is always worthwhile taking trouble with this. In embroidering this sampler and making it up into a folder you will learn a great deal, and make something which is useful and decorative. The sampler in the illustration was the worker's first project, with it she set herself a very sound standard. If you succeed in doing the same, your thought and effort will not have been in vain.

Begin by tacking out two rectangular shapes measuring $11\frac{1}{2}$ in. high by $3\frac{1}{2}$ in. wide on the canvas, leaving 5 in. between each shape.

Fig 48 (*opposite*)   Sampler by Margaret Wheeler

The stitch sampler should be embroidered first. The arrangement of the chosen stitches should be carefully planned to ensure that each is seen to the best advantage; some will be worked all in one colour, making a smooth or textured surface, others will use two colours to make an all-over pattern or a chequer pattern.

Choose your colours with great care, so that you have something light, something dark, and one other colour of a tone between light and dark. The choice of white, drab olive, and a soft turquoise blue for the sampler in fig. 48 was a very happy one; another satisfactory choice would be off-white, dark green, and lime; or cream, coffee brown and terracotta. Colours such as scarlet or shocking pink are too dominant for this purpose and should be avoided. Black is too dark, and makes it difficult to see the individual stitches.

The embroidery can be worked directly, without preliminary tacking (basting), or drawing of each unit on the canvas, by proceeding in the following way. Work 2 rows of cross stitch down the centre of the rectangle and 2 rows across the top of the shape. Immediately underneath, and on either side of the centre, work your first 2 stitch units, $1\frac{1}{2}$ in. square. Work two rows of cross stitch underneath these to separate them from the next units, and repeat this procedure until all 12 are completed. Work 3 rows of cross stitch under the bottom units; remove the tacked (basted) outline of the rectangle and complete the panel by working 2 more rows down each side of the sampler. This cross stitch frame should be worked in either the dark colour or the middle tone colour.

The outline of the building motif, and the position of window shapes, should be tacked out on the canvas and then the embroidery worked as directly as possible.

The sketches on the opposite page show how easily a rectangular shape can be varied to make alternative building motifs. The size of these is exactly half of that required for the sampler, so if you want to use either of them as your starting point, tack it on to the canvas twice this size. But before doing so, try out one or two variations for yourself on a piece of graph paper, and use one of your own if possible. As long as you keep it very simple and well proportioned you cannot go far wrong.

The extreme simplicity of the shape of the building allows the maximum scope for using the stitches to enrich and embellish, which is as it should be; too complicated or elaborate a shape would force them into trying to 'draw', which is not their proper function here.

Fig 49 (*opposite*)

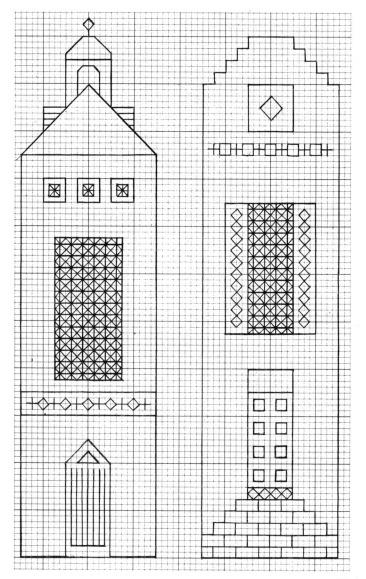

Fig 50   Smyrna cross stitch
worked in a chequer pattern

Arrange your colour so that the building shape stands out well
against the background, and your stitches so that the plain and
patterned areas are well contrasted. A careful study of the sampler
(fig. 48) will help you to do this successfully. Notice too how the
choice and arrangement of the stitches gives effective contrast of
scale, as well as of pattern and texture; the cross stitch on the main
body of the building sets off the larger and more decorative
stitches, giving them full value, while the close-knit texture of
the upright cross stitch on the background enhances the whole.
When you have decided the colour for the background and the
main area of the building, it is a good idea to begin by embroidering the motif, adding the background stitchery as it becomes
helpful to see the building against its colour and texture. It is not a
good idea to embroider the background all round the motif first,
as, however careful you are, there is a risk of pulling the canvas
and leaving yourself with a puckered area in the middle.

As you have worked on a frame and neither panel is large, the
finished embroidery will be flat and in good shape, so that it will
not be necessary to stretch it before mounting (matting). However,
before removing it from the frame you can ensure the maximum
flatness in the following way if you wish. Make sure that the
canvas is straight and taut on the frame. Lay the work down with
the reverse side upwards, and thoroughly dampen with a sponge
and water; allow it to dry off for about twenty-four hours and then
remove the work from the frame by cutting the canvas $1\frac{1}{2}$ in.
beyond the edge of the embroidery on all sides.

If you have used the edges of the canvas for experimenting with
the stitches, save any of these which may be useful for reference
and mount them on cardboard for your embroidery notebook, or as
a small sampler. The remainder of the canvas will be removed
from the webbing by carefully snipping the stitches.

Mounting (matting)·the sampler

A sheet of mounting card (matboard)
A Stanley knife and a steel ruler
A metal plate or other hard surface for cutting on
Copydex (Sobo in U.S.) and Sellotape (Scotch Tape in U.S.)
A pair of strong scissors and a pencil
1 yd of 2-in. wide adhesive carpet tape in black or other suitable
colour

1 Four pieces of mounting card, each measuring $7\frac{1}{2}$ in. × $15\frac{1}{2}$ in.
are needed for making the mount (mat). Two are for framing the
embroidery and 2 for making the outside cover. Mounting card
is made in good colours; you will probably find a medium or dark
grey suitable and safe, but you should choose carefully, with your
particular work in mind. Cut these 4 pieces with a Stanley knife;
never try to cut mounts with scissors.
2 By measuring 2 in. in from each edge, draw lightly in pencil
a shape measuring $11\frac{1}{2}$ in. × $3\frac{1}{2}$ in. on 2 of the cut cards (mat-
boards). This is to be cut out, to leave a 'window' frame for your
embroidery.
3 Cut out these shapes with the steel ruler placed between the
Stanley knife and the outside edges of the mount (mat). This will
prevent it being damaged, should the knife slip.
4 Place the cut out mounts (mats) on the embroidery panels, and
when in place secure the edges with Sellotape (Scotch Tape) on
the back of the card (mat).
5 Take the other 2 cards (mats), and a piece of adhesive tape $16\frac{1}{2}$
in. long. Lay the tape with the adhesive side uppermost. Mark a
line across the top and the bottom $\frac{1}{2}$ in. from the edge. On each of
these lines make marks $\frac{3}{4}$ in. in from either side of the tape. Take
each piece of card (matboard) in turn and lay it, right side downwards, on the adhesive tape, with the corners level with the line
top and bottom and against the marks $\frac{3}{4}$ in. in from the sides. A
space of about $\frac{1}{2}$ in. will be left between the 2 cards, in the centre.
6 Smooth the edges of the cards (mats) so that they adhere to the
tape then turn the edges of the adhesive tape over the cards, at the
top and bottom. Cut another piece of tape measuring 15 in., and
stick this down the centre, covering the area of exposed adhesive
and the turned over edges, to make a neat and firm finish.
7 Cover the two cards (mats) evenly and not too thinly with

Fig 51 The mounted (matted) sampler

Copydex (Sobo in U.S.) and place the two mounted (matted) panels carefully on this, so that the edges match perfectly. The inside edges will show the $\frac{1}{2}$ in. or so of black tape between them at the centre. Leave flat under pressure for about an hour before folding it, and you should have a serviceable and attractive folder sampler.

Stitch motifs and patterns

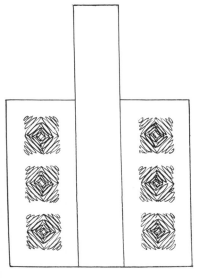

Fig 52 The embroidered units can be used to decorate a bag like this, either separately or in bands. Choose a firm fabric like sailcloth for the bag

Fig 53 Simple motifs can be built up with stitches. This one is made with units of seven stitches arranged in a kind of mosaic

Fig 54 The units can be repeated to make a belt, or an embroidered panel or yoke for a dress.
Raffene or Perlita can be used for the centre stitches, and wool or other contrasting thread for the triangular corners

Fig 55   The motif can be applied in separate units to decorate a pocket or make a belt
Below is another idea for an embroidered belt.

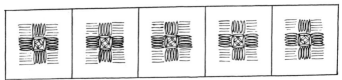

Fig 56   The rice stitch in the centre is worked in synthetic raffia, the long stitches are worked in wool (yarn).

Fig 57

Fig 58

Fig 57   A suggestion for an
embroidered belt

Fig 58   An embroidered pocket, yoke or
panel can lend distinction to a simple
dress. By Jan Beaney. Reproduced by
courtesy of the Embroiderers' Guild,
London

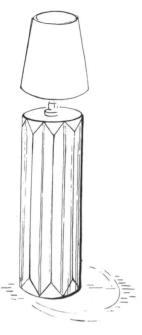

Fig 59

Fig 60   Detail of embroidery for a lamp base by
Dorothy Falconer. The photograph on the title page
shows the complete embroidered design. The rich
pattern of stitches is made mainly by cross stitch,
Smyrna and diagonal stitch worked with wool
(yarn) and cotton embroidery thread. Long-legged
cross stitch, between the rows of eye stitch, and
diagonal Florentine on the background are worked
in goldfingering

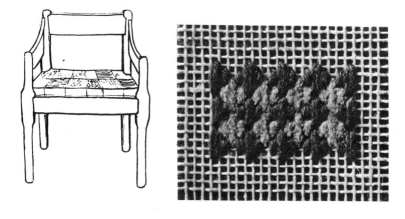

Fig 61   An idea for an embroidered chair pad. Hungarian stitch embroidered in chenille yarn and woollen thread makes an attractive pattern; many other canvas stitches can be used in the same way to make pattern, and experiments can be made with all kinds of threads. By Jan Beaney. Reproduced by courtesy of the Embroiderers' Guild, London

Fig 62   An alternative suggestion – divide the pad into geometric shapes and introduce a contrasting stitch or pattern

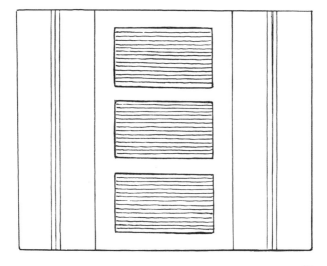

Design

A knowledge of the materials at your disposal, and an understanding of their proper use, is the first essential in learning to design successfully for any craft. This comes through practice in working with them, and by trial and error.

From the experiments you have made with threads and stitches, you will have learned a lot about the individual qualities of each, and their potentialities for making texture and pattern. You will have experienced the discipline of working on the counted thread of the canvas, and discovered how it governs the character of the embroidery, giving it a pleasing formality.

The stitches can be used to make surface pattern and texture, or arranged in such a way as to make separate units or motifs – which can be repeated or combined to make border or ground patterns. All these have a specifically-geometric character, and illustrate the way in which the limitations imposed by the canvas ground, once understood and accepted, are a help rather than a hindrance in designing for canvas embroidery.

The term design includes shape, colour, tone, texture and pattern; contrast (of light and dark, large and small shapes), and the unity and balance of all these elements. If you have made a sampler on the lines suggested on page 53 you have already had some practice with all these aspects of design, and are equipped with some useful knowledge and experience of your craft, from which to begin designing.

Planning a cushion

A cushion like the one illustrated on page 70 would make an excellent first exercise in design. It is a more ambitious piece of work than the folder sampler, it provides plenty of opportunity for a more adventurous use of stitches and colour, and it gives practice in designing with shapes.

Geometric shapes are a good beginning for design for canvas embroidery; the sketches (figs 63–5) opposite show the development of a pattern from an arrangement of squares and rectangles. Look at the diagrams and embroidered motifs on the next pages; they show some ways in which these familiar, basic shapes can be used and developed with stitchery into interesting units and motifs. It would be a good idea to spend a little time exploring on these lines, before beginning to plan a pattern for the cushion.

Colour need not be limited to the same extent as it was for the first sampler, but it is just as important to choose it with care and discrimination; the shapes as well as stitch patterns and textures

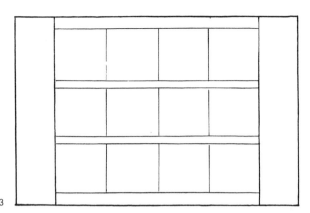
Fig 63

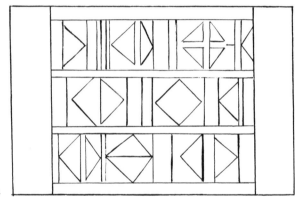
Fig 64

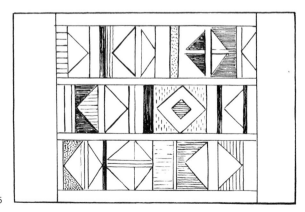
Fig 65

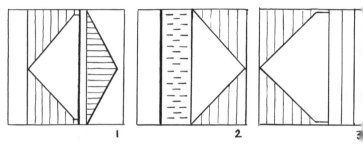

Fig 66   Three ways to divide up a square to make pattern

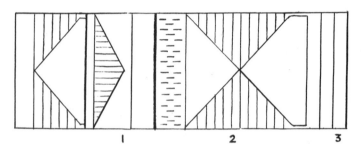

Fig 67   An arrangement of the three squares to make a more developed pattern

Fig 68   The pattern worked out in attractively varied stitches and well-contrasted texture and tone

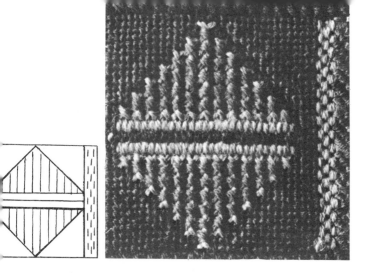

Fig 69   Fig 70

Fig 71   Another arrangement of basic shapes to make pattern

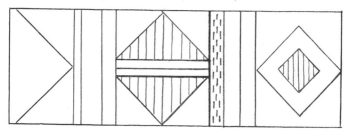

should be considered this time. It can be as bright and gay as you like, but if you use too many different colours the result will be an incoherent muddle. A better way is to use different shades of one colour, then you can add one other colour closely related to this, and another which makes a decided contrast. In this way you will more easily work out a harmonious and balanced arrangement of colour and tone.

The cushion in the illustration (p. 70) used a range of green, from very dark to light emerald, a dark blue and a rich, deep blue, and for contrast, a vivid lime green and a little pale gold. The threads are crewel wool (yarn) and stranded embroidery thread. Another scheme could be worked from a range of red, from dark wine to light pink, with the addition of some purples, and, for contrast, a little bright orange.

When you have chosen your colours, and worked out one or two motifs, you will have a better idea of how to use these and other similar motifs to make the cushion design. Take care to have a balanced arrangement of squares and rectangles and subsidiary shapes, and develop your plan on graph paper in the same way as shown in fig. 65. A sound foundation will enable you to develop the pattern of stitch, colour and shape as freely and directly as in the case of your experimental motifs; this will give your finished design vitality and freshness, for every stitch will be informed with your thought and particular intention.

The cushion measures 12 in.×16 in. and instructions for framing-up a piece of canvas of the size required for making it are given on page 23. For information about making up the cushion see page 95.

Suggestions for planning the back of the cushion are given on page 71. The design is again developed from the square and the rectangle, but the shapes are larger and the pattern is much simpler in contrast to the front. Colour and texture will be the main considerations in working this side of the cushion. Let it be predominantly in tones of one colour, with some of the closely-related colour, but use the contrasting colour sparingly, if at all. In this way, it will help to set off the diversity of pattern and colour of the front of the cushion, so that as a whole it is a well and attractively-designed article.

If you find that, in spite of all your care, some stitches worked in the darker colours allow the canvas to show through, you can paint the area to be covered with waterproof ink of a similar colour to the thread, before embroidering; this is a perfectly legitimate procedure on all such occasions.

Fig 72   The City by Mary Hall, a choir stall cushion

Fig 73   Donkey by Ruth Hodge, an embroidered wall panel

69

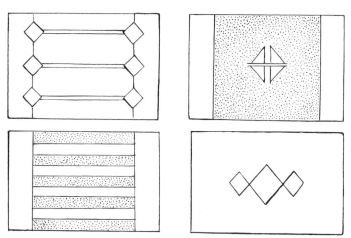

Fig 75   Ideas for the back of the cushion

Fig 74 (*opposite*)   Cushion cover by Daphne Green. A design developed from simple basic shapes – the rectangle, the square, and the component shapes, the diamond and triangle

Fig 76   Stool top by Norah Gibbon embroidered with crewel wool (yarn) on a fine linen canvas in cross stitch, upright Gobelin, star stitch and stem stitch. The satisfying arrangement of the diamond shapes is enhanced by the varied stitch textures and the well-balanced tone values. (See also page 27.)

More about shapes

The rich and varied pattern of the cushion cover grew and developed from a carefully-planned arrangement of squares and rectangles and their subsidiary shapes – the diamond and the triangle – all of which are suggested by the geometric nature of the canvas itself. The stitches, too, being worked horizontally, vertically, or diagonally on the canvas, marry naturally with these shapes.

From the folder sampler (fig. 48) and other illustrations in this book, it can be seen how readily these same basic shapes can be arranged to make a pattern or design representing buildings. Fig. 41 is a simple and straightforward example, with attractive variation of texture and stitch pattern and well-balanced tone. Fig. 92, which is worked on a finer canvas, shows a more subtle and sophisticated pattern of shapes and stitches.

The more complex shapes of animals and birds can be simplified and developed from the same basic shapes without losing any of their character and liveliness. The sketches on the opposite page were made with a brush on graph paper; all the shapes are worked out on the three directions natural to the canvas. If you will make a few experiments for yourself, you will discover how the motifs practically design themselves once you begin working in this way. The spots, stripes, and other characteristic features make lovely pattern, and worked in gay colours with an imaginative use of thread and stitch, these geometric animals and birds make engaging nursery panels.

The dove with the olive branch (fig. 78) is worked on a cushion for a choir stall in a church. It was the embroiderer's first experience of working directly and creatively with shapes and stitches. The size and position of the dove on the cushion was planned on graph paper, and then the outline of the bird was tacked (basted) onto the canvas; all the other shapes were determined as the work progressed. The result is a perfect example of embroidery on canvas demonstrating very plainly all the elements of good design (see page 64, paragraph four).

Good design is always an integral part of the article, it is not something separate which is applied to it, or imposed upon it. It grows from an imaginative use of the materials, the shapes, and the stitches, and it takes account of the size, shape, and purpose of the article, so that, from the beginning, it is thought of as a whole.

Fig 77 (*opposite*)

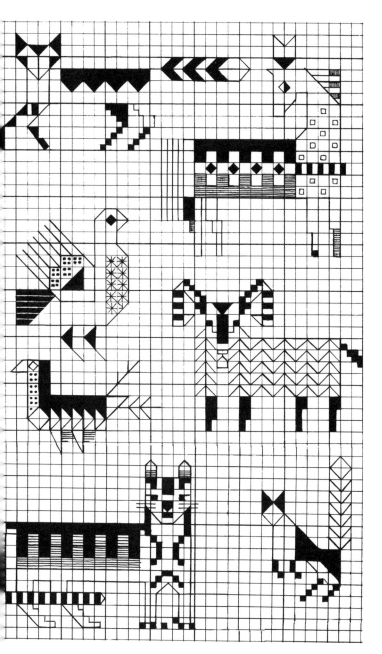

73

There is no easy formula for creating a design; it is the result of knowledge of the materials and stitches; understanding of their use; and of the requirements of the article; thoughtful application and practice.

Designs can be planned in a number of ways, and with practice and experience you will find the one which suits you. You may find more freedom in expressing your ideas with shapes cut out of paper; these can be arranged, and re-arranged, within your given shape, until they make a satisfactory pattern or composition. Another way is to 'doodle' with a thick thread on the surface of the canvas; as the shapes appear they can be pinned in place, then re-adjusted until they are as you want them. The design can be painted on the canvas from the outline made by the thread.

As you become more sensitive to shape, pattern and texture, all so essential a part of canvas embroidery and design, you will become more aware of the wealth of shape, pattern and texture around you – in everyday things and in nature. Look at the pattern of shape and texture to be found on tree barks, some of them have an unexpected and close affinity to the shapes required by your embroidery. Sketches or photographs of these will provide valuable ideas for design. Patterns on pebbles and shells and snails, the shadow patterns of leaves and stems or tree trunks, and the markings on animals and reptiles, and flowers; all these, and many others, are a rich source of ideas and inspiration.

An embroidery notebook

An embroidery notebook is most valuable for reference, and is enjoyable to make. Samples of canvas and threads, and other useful materials, can be collected and put into the book, with notes about prices, widths, and suppliers. New stitches can be recorded on a sampler, as you learn them, and included when complete – perhaps you can make diagrams to go with them. The experiments you make with new threads, stitches, beads, glass and so on, can be mounted (matted), and will make attractive and interesting pages. Sketches and exercises in design on graph paper; more freely-drawn studies of shells, birds, buildings or animals; photographs of all kinds of things; studies done in museums and postcard reproductions of embroideries, pottery, metal work; pressed flowers and leaves; feathers – all these could find a place in your notebook, and you will discover many others in the process of making it.

Two thicknesses of mounting card (matboard) glued together

Fig 78   Dove by Daphne Green. Cushion embroidered in crewel wool (yarn) on 14-mesh canvas
Fig 79   This sketch could be adapted for a number of purposes

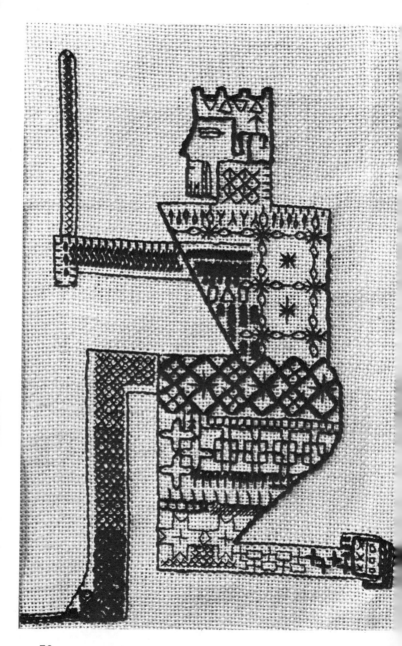

Figs 80 and 81   Pages from a notebook. The black-work figure is admirably designed for embroidery on the counted thread, and could easily be adapted for canvas embroidery. Fig 81   Sketch by Judith Parker

Fig 80 (*opposite*)   Figure embroidered in black work by Ann Erli

will make firm covers, and a good size is about 10 in. × 12 in. Sheets of thinner cardboard in a variety of colours make attractive inside pages. These can be bought in packets ready cut (see list of suppliers on page 102). The notebook can be held together by a cord threaded through holes punched in each page. Eyelets will give a professional finish to the holes on the covers. If the cord can be hand-made and finished off with tassels, so much the better.

Fig 82 Detail of panel by Jean Hayne. Tent and fan stitches have been used to work the background of this panel. The design is carried out in gold leather, gold cords, creosoted string in double knot stitch, and goldfingering yarn. One area has been cut out and stained glass placed behind the canvas

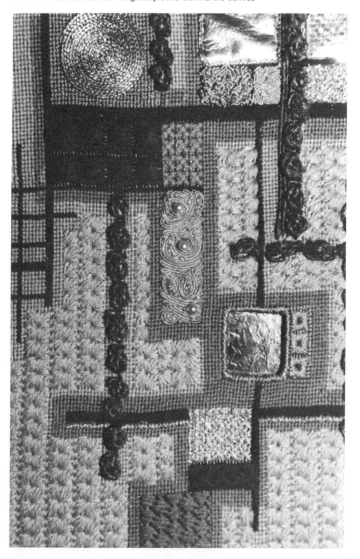

Surface stitchery and applied shapes

It is always stimulating to experiment with new ways of working, as well as with new kinds of threads and materials; and once the discipline of the counted thread has been thoroughly learned and understood, you can begin to explore on more unorthodox lines.

The illustration on page 78 suggests several new and exciting possibilities. Surface stitchery has been used to introduce linear and textural richness, and to lend emphasis to the design. On this panel, double knot stitch has been worked in string that has been treated with creosote (a wood tar derivative) to make coarse raised lines on the canvas embroidery; it has also been couched in flat lines. Gold cords of different kinds have been sewn down – in spirals to make circles, and, more freely, to make rich textures.

The attractive use of french knots in fig. 84 not only provides a close, raised texture, but enhances the effectiveness of the gold kid and the beads, and helps them to become a part of the essential fabric.

It should be observed that in each case the surface stitchery is an integral part of the design, not something which has been added just to give effect. In making similar experiments you will discover more ways of using these and other surface stitches. For example, split stitch can be worked freely to give firm or fine line, and heavy or delicate textural effects; fly stitch worked in different sizes and different thicknesses of thread gives interest on a ground of tent stitch.

Simple shapes cut out in suede, leather, gold and silver kid, or felt, can be padded and easily applied to the embroidered surface, as they will not fray. With their smooth, shiny or matt surfaces, they contrast well with the texture and pattern of the stitches, and have an immensely enriching effect when used with under-standing and discrimination (as can be seen in figs 82 and 84). The shapes should always be suggested by the canvas and the design, and should never be arbitrarily imposed.

Cutting holes

To cut shapes out of the canvas in order to use the holes as 'windows' for coloured glass, metal, or other such alien material, seems a much more daring innovation. Try it out for yourself; you will be surprised how exciting and invigorating this sort of experiment can be.

The panel in fig. 82 illustrates the successful integration of coloured glass into a design which is for a purely decorative

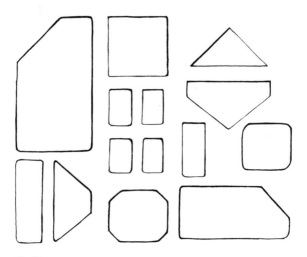

Fig 83

Fig 84 (*opposite*) Shell by Nelly Mansfield. This design was inspired by a skeleton shell. It is worked on a background of Hungarian stitch embroidered with wool (yarn) and goldfingering yarn. Goldfingering outlines the shell, too, and gold kid is applied to the centre, which is further enriched with French knots and beads. Smyrna and tent stitches are used for working the rest of the shell

purpose. As in the case of the applied gold kid on the same panel, the cut shapes conform to the demands of the canvas and the design, and have been used with great discernment and discretion, so that there is no feeling of inappropriateness or disparity between the glass and the surrounding stitchery, but each enhances the other in a compelling harmony.

On your experimental pieces you can practise cutting a variety of shapes (fig. 83) and covering the cut edges of the canvas. Always cut your hole a little smaller than your glass or metal, to keep it in place. It requires a certain amount of skill and perseverance to get a perfectly firm, even edge, as the canvas frays easily when it is cut, but you can help to prevent this in the following way: paint the outline of the shape on the canvas and then lightly brush a colourless liquid glue (any ordinary liquid glue) over the area to be cut, and the painted outline. Allow this to dry thoroughly, then very carefully cut out the shape with sharp, pointed scissors. The gummed threads should give a crisp, firm edge when cut, which can be covered by overcasting over two threads of the canvas. Further decoration can be added to the outline of the shape by sewing a cord or threads around it if you wish. The glass or metal is fastened onto the back of the canvas and kept in place by taking stitches backwards and forwards across it.

Beads, jewels, and metal threads

The embroiderer today has at her disposal beads, jewels, and metal threads in such profusion and variety that the problem is often to avoid an over-enthusiastic use of too many in one piece of work. The small gold beads which have been introduced among the french knots in fig. 84 perfectly echo the richness of the gold kid, and this is a very suitable and restrained use of beads with embroidery. Generally speaking, they should be used to give textural contrast and interest, and emphasis to some part of the design, so they should be grouped together rather than scattered all over the surface. Larger beads can be used singly, or in twos or threes, and spaced out with greater deliberation (see fig. 89).

Fig. 86 shows a lovely and appropriately-jewelled cross, the focal point of a panel of otherwise mainly sombre colour. The central jewel is surrounded with bugle beads and sequins to give a wonderfully rich effect. Stitches in goldfingering have been taken across the jewels, and this has been used most successfully on the background as well. When beads and jewels are used with understanding, for a reason and a purpose, so that they become a necessary part of the design, they can add beauty and richness, which is complemented both by the matt texture of woollen threads (yarns) and the discreet shine of some metal threads. As in the case of the glass used in the panel (fig. 82), they must become an integral part of the whole work, otherwise the temptation to use them had better be resisted. Of course, your intention may sometimes be to enjoy yourself with a less serious and more frivolous piece of work, and to break all the rules. This is often a very profitable exercise, as well as being fun, and can teach you a great deal about the dos and don'ts of beads and jewels, or other kinds of innovations that may occur to you. One word of warning: learn the rules first!

A variety of gold, silver, aluminium and Lurex threads and cords can be worked on canvas, and with a little practice you will discover how well they combine with all kinds of other threads, to give lovely effects. Goldfingering, which is an untarnishable yarn, is one of the most satisfactory and rewarding: it is a cool gold which makes a pleasant rich, and not too shiny, texture (fig. 86), and is particularly good in combination with woollen threads (yarns). Lurex threads and cords, too, are untarnishable; they can be worked into the canvas mesh among other threads, or the coarser cords can be couched on the surface of the embroidery as in fig. 82. Some other fine cords and threads which are suitable are not untarnishable, but they should not be rejected on this

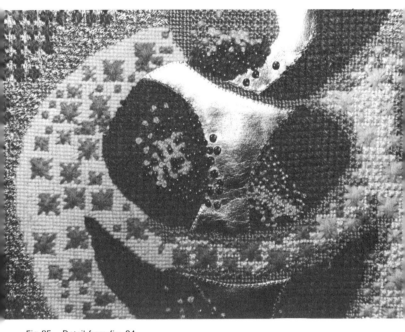

Fig 85   Detail from fig. 84

account, for a tarnished thread can be quite as lovely, in a more subtle way.

Only by practice, and trial and error, will you discover how to use all these threads, beads and jewels successfully; many of them are quite inexpensive and you will find the names and addresses of suppliers on page 102.

Fig 86   Jewel surrounded by bugle beads and sequins on a cross of Smyrna and tent stitches. Detail from a panel by Teresa Blackall

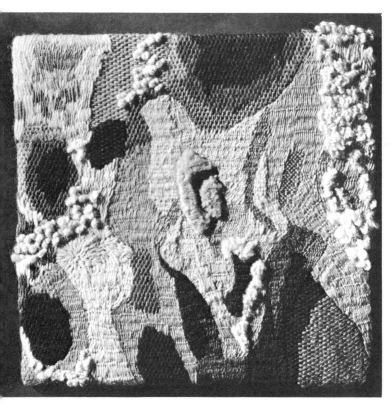

Fig 87 This small panel by Janet Payne worked on fine canvas shows rich and unusual texture made by the threads and stitches. French knots, tufting and looped wool (yarn) have been used

Fig 88 An interesting experiment in which threads of the canvas are used in working, together with wools (yarns) and other fibres

Fig 89   Texture, by Mary Rhodes

Embroidered panels

Embroidered panels and wall-hangings allow the maximum scope for experimenting with threads, materials and stitches, and enjoying shapes, colours and texture; for there are fewer restricting practical considerations than with articles which are subject to use, and wear and tear.

The illustrations show a number of different approaches. The engaging panel (fig. 73), like the dove cushion (fig. 78), was the embroiderer's first experience of working directly and creatively with stitches, and was planned and worked in exactly the same way as the dove cushion. The arrangement and proportion of the shapes within the given rectangle, and in relation to each other, is most satisfactory and harmonious, and this is enhanced by skilfully-balanced tone. This panel has great simplicity, and the enjoyment of stitch pattern and texture, and beautiful glowing – but controlled – colour, is very evident. *A Village in the Sun* (fig. 92 and detail, fig. 26) too, is concerned with the enjoyment and exploitation of stitch patterns and shapes, and this has resulted in a most accomplished and interesting design.

A more experimental approach can be seen in figs 82, 84 and 87, and we have already studied and appreciated the successful way in which surface stitchery and some unusual threads and materials have been introduced and combined with the canvas stitchery. There is plenty of scope for adventure and exploration here.

The bold colours and angular shapes of the design on the opposite page give an impression of depth and richness, like the facets of a jewel; there is too, a scintillating quality about the whole thing which is emphasized by the long surface stitches. In this panel, as in all the examples mentioned, there is a great economy of shape. In the same way that too many different colours will make a design incoherent, so too many different shapes will make confusion. Try to discover the basic shapes from which these designs are developed, you will be surprised to find how few they are, perhaps only a rectangle, and its component shapes, a square, diamond, and triangle, as can be plainly traced in fig. 92.

The panel *Artichoke* on page 90 is worked on jute canvas. The interpretation is striking and spontaneous, and the use of tent stitch worked in different kinds and thicknesses of wool (yarn) is particularly interesting. Here the preoccupation is with texture and colour, rather than with shape.

Fig 90 (*opposite*)   Panel, designed by Mary Rhodes, worked by Sally Right

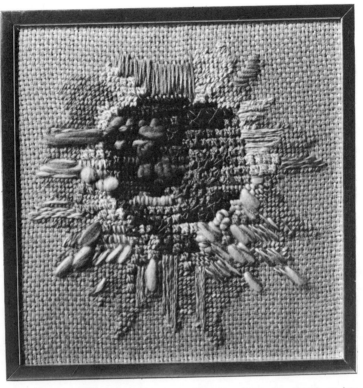

Fig 91   Artichoke by Diana Springall. Embroidery in woollen threads on jute canvas

Fig 92 (*opposite*)   *A Village in the Sun* by May Thurgood. A small panel worked with vegetable-dyed wools (yarns) and silk in many stitches including tent, cross, eyelet, Hungarian, and upright Gobelin. The strong, simple shapes, striking tone contrasts, and sensitive use of Florentine stitch on the background, all help to convey the impression of light, warmth, and a gently stirring breeze. Notice the importance of the horizontal lines of the boats and the two vertical masts in stabilizing the whole design

Fig 93 Cock by Barbara Hudson. Embroidered with crewel wools (yarns) on single linen canvas in cross, upright cross, reverse tent, bricking, upright Gobelin and diagonal Florentine stitches on a ground of tent stitch

Contemporary interiors provide wonderful settings for the rich colour and texture of embroidery, and a panel or wall-hanging in canvas embroidery can make an appropriate and lovely focal point.

As with other things, the mounting or making up of a panel or hanging is an important part of the job, and you should spend time and thought on this. If necessary, have it done professionally.

92

Transferring a design to the canvas

One of the best ways to prepare a design for canvas embroidery is by drawing it, actual size, on graph paper. The centre lines, vertically and horizontally, should be marked on the paper and the canvas. The design can then be transferred in one of the following ways:

1 Draw the outline of the design on the paper with a bold line in Indian ink. Place the drawing under the canvas, matching the centre lines. Keep both in position by tacking or with weights. The drawing will show through sufficiently for you to paint the design onto the canvas with waterproof ink. This is done most easily just before the prepared canvas is put onto the frame. If the canvas is already framed-up, books of an appropriate thickness can be placed under the drawing to keep it close to the canvas and to give a firm surface on which to paint.

2 The design can be transferred from the paper by measurement, and tacked (basted) or painted onto the canvas.

3 If the graph paper has the same number of squares to the inch as the canvas has holes to the inch, the design can be transferred by counting.

A design can be worked out directly on the canvas by tacking (basting), and trial and error.

Sometimes a design is prepared from cut-out paper shapes. In this case it may be possible to lay the shapes on the canvas and paint or tack round them.

Footnote Make quite sure that any ink which is used on the canvas is waterproof. Do not use paint.

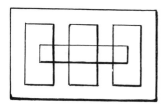 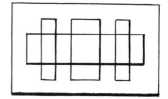

Fig 94   Two suggestions for hassocks

Stretching the embroidery

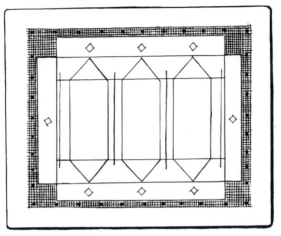

Fig 95 Canvas pinned (tacked) out for stretching

Embroidery which has been worked on a frame and kept at an even tension should remain flat and in shape, and require no actual stretching before mounting or making up, but it is, nevertheless, a good idea to freshen it up and ensure maximum flatness in the way suggested on page 56. If it has been worked in the hand, or for some other reason is badly puckered or pulled out of shape, it will be necessary to stretch it as follows:

Lay two or three sheets of clean blotting paper on a flat wooden board and place the work on this with the reverse side up. Slightly dampen the back of the embroidery by gently dabbing it with a soft cloth. When this is done, remove it, and thoroughly dampen the sheets of blotting paper. Then put the embroidery on top of this with the right side up. Place one of the selvedge edges so that it is true (flush) with the edge of the board. Measure the distance between the edge of the embroidery and the edge of the board, and when it is quite accurate, pin firmly in place with rustless drawing pins (thumbtacks) or upholstery nails, at least 1 in. from the edge of the embroidery. The canvas is fairly flexible at this stage, and can be pulled firmly but carefully back into shape. Pin the side opposite the first, checking that the four corners are square, and measuring as before. Then proceed in the same way to pin out and measure the remaining two sides. The embroidery should be left pinned out over the damp blotting paper for at least twenty-four hours, when it should be thoroughly dry and firmly in shape again. If you are having your work made up by an upholsterer, he will usually undertake the stretching as well, but it will add considerably to the cost.

Making up a cushion

Your work can literally be made or marred by the making up of the finished article. It is most important that the necessary time and care be given to doing this well. Before removing the embroidery from the frame, dampen it, and leave for twenty-four hours according to the instructions on page 56, to make sure that it is flat and in shape. This greatly assists the making up (finishing).

Inexpensive cushion pads, 12 in. × 16 in., can be bought (see list of suppliers, page 102), or you can make your own with un-bleached calico and kapok in the following way:

1 Cut two rectangles of calico measuring $12\frac{1}{2}$ in. × $16\frac{1}{2}$ in. plus $\frac{1}{2}$-in. turnings. Machine stitch all round, leaving an opening of about 6 in. on one side. Turn right side out. The calico case is made this much larger to ensure that when it is stuffed the pad well fills the embroidered cushion cover.

2 Tease out the kapok so that no lumps remain, distribute it evenly to make a firm, flat pad, pressing it well into the corners; do not overfill it. When it is sufficiently firm, sew up the opening.

3 Cut the embroidery from the frame leaving enough canvas for 1-in. turnings. A piped (corded) edge will give a good finish to the cushion. The colour should match one of the colours in the embroidery and the material should not be too thick or bulky. Number 3 piping ($\frac{1}{8}$-in. diameter cording) is the size for cushions.

4 Cut the crossway pieces (bias strips) $1\frac{1}{2}$ in. wide, from the true cross (bias) of the material. Stitch the sections together to make a length the total measurement of the four sides, plus 1 in. for the join. Seam the join and press open with an iron, then trim to $\frac{1}{4}$ in.

The piping cord (cording) can be cut to the exact length required and the two ends brought together and stitched; or it can be spliced and the join made neat and secure by winding a thread around it; in this case allow an extra 1 in.

Fold the strip of material over the piping cord (cording), and pin in place before tacking (basting); then machine stitch with the piping foot (on U.S. machines, use the zipper foot), or back stitch by hand.

Pin the continuous length of piping (cording) to the right side of the front of the cushion cover, edge to edge, and tack (baste). Snip the turnings at the corners, machine or hand stitch all round.

Place the two right sides of the cushion cover together, pin and tack (baste) round three sides and 1 in. round the corners of the fourth side, as close as possible to the piping (cording). Stitch by hand or machine. Press, then turn the right side out.

Carefully insert the cushion pad through the opening, pressing well into the corners, pin the opening and slip stitch together.

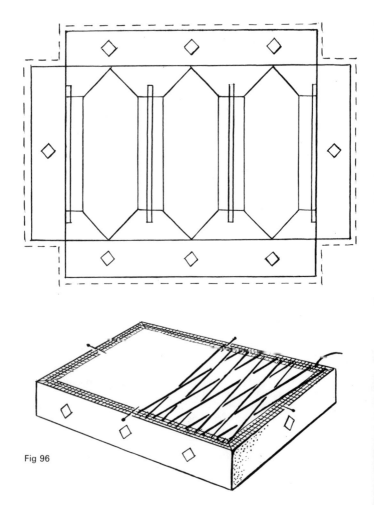

Fig 96

Making up a kneeler (hassock)

A kneeler (hassock), and a cushion or chair pad with embroidered sides, can be worked all in one piece, which simplifies the making up (finishing). Tack (baste) out the whole shape on the canvas, as shown in fig. 97. When the embroidery is complete, remove it from the frame and cut it out, leaving enough canvas for $\frac{3}{4}$-in. turnings. Sew up the corners on the wrong side, carefully press (iron) the turnings flat and turn right side out.

The hassock can be made up (finished) professionally, by an upholsterer, or you can make it up yourself. It is important that this should be well done, not only for the sake of your embroidery, but because it must stand up to a good deal of wear and tear. A piece of foam rubber or Dunlopillo (foam rubber or resilient plastic foam in US) makes an excellent filling, and is easy to manage. It is obtainable in different thicknesses and the supplier will usually cut shapes to your requirements. It is a good idea to have the rubber pad cut about a $\frac{1}{2}$ in. bigger than your actual measurements, to ensure that the embroidered cover is well filled out. The rubber pad should be covered with a calico case made to the same measurements as the hassock.

Slip the embroidered cover over the rubber pad, and if necessary stuff the corners with a little cotton wadding. The corners can be kept firmly in position by taking a stitch through the calico or rubber. If the top of the hassock appears to need extra filling, one or two layers of cotton wadding or felt can be stitched to the calico case under the embroidery.

Then place the hassock face downwards and turn over the edges of the canvas and pin. These can be stitched down to the calico, or you can lace from edge to edge, first the long sides, then the shorter, with a strong linen thread or carpet thread. Be careful not to pull the kneeler (hassock) out of shape in doing this.

To cover the underneath side of the hassock, cut out a rectangle of glazed hessian or upholsterers' linen, press (iron) the turnings, and pin in place. Then hem all round, sewing in a ring for hanging if necessary.

Fig 97   Lamb by Priscilla Leonard. This motif is embroidered on an altar cushion with crewel wool (yarn) in cross, upright cross, Smyrna, Parisian, tent, and flat stitch

Figs 98 and 99   Two wedding hassocks by Norah Edwards and Barbara Hudson worked in white, light and dark blue with a touch of pale lime green. The unicorn signifies chastity and the sun and moon symbolize respectively the masculine and the feminine

In conclusion

The aim of this book has been to encourage you to discover the simple pleasure of using stitches and shapes to create something personal and unique, and in so doing to experience a deeper satisfaction and delight in your work. If you have been able to do this, you will have realized some of the hidden potentials within yourself, and enjoyed not only the results of your thought and effort, but, in however small a way, the process of creation itself. How much more worthwhile all this is than the monotonous embroidering of one stitch all over a piece of canvas with a commercially-prepared picture or pattern printed on it.

You may feel that too much stress has been laid upon the discipline and demands of the canvas, especially as you become more aware of the new and adventurous freedom which is apparent in every kind of embroidery today. You will be eager to experiment with all kinds of new threads and materials, and to explore new ways of using the conventional means in order to express your expanding ideas. All this is as it should be. But it is only through a thorough knowledge and understanding of your basic materials, gained through patient and persevering work with them, that you will develop the confidence and ability to enable you to experiment successfully.

The initial delight of discovering how to create with the stitches and shapes will show itself in your work, and your early pieces will have a freshness and originality which is entirely your own. The particular and individual quality which is the essence of your work makes it quite unlike that of anyone else; this is the valuable thing. As you become more experienced and confident, try to go on working and developing your own ideas in your own way; while, at the same time, learning all you can from the work of other people. It will provide you with a lifetime of interest and enjoyment.

Fig 100   London by Miriam Bawden. A delightful detail, depicting the Tower of London. This very individual piece of work shows great simplicity of design, and a lovely variety of stitch and texture. The background is worked in double straight cross, diagonal stitch has been used in a number of different ways, and the small amount of tent stitch on the buildings gives enough contrast to clarify the pattern and add significance to the shapes

List of suppliers (England)

Mace and Nairn, Embroidery Specialists, 89 Crane Street, Salisbury, Wiltshire (For every conceivable requirement. Catalogue sent on request)

The Royal School of Needlework, 25 Princes Gate, London SW7 (Linen embroidery canvas of every kind, crewel and tapestry wools, other embroidery threads)

Harrods Ltd, Knightsbridge, London SW1 (Linen embroidery canvas, crewel and tapestry wools, some other embroidery threads including metal threads, embroidery frames)

The Needlewoman Shop, Regent Street, London W1 (Every kind of embroidery thread, embroidery frames, rug canvas, but only double-embroidery canvas)

The Bead Shop, 53 South Molton Street, London W1 (Beads, pearls, etc.)

The Weavers House, Royal Wilton Carpet Factory, Wilton, Wiltshire (Carpet wool – thrums)

Jacksons, Rug Craft Centre, Croft Mill, Hebden Bridge, Yorkshire (2-ply thrums, carpet yarn in lengths or hanks, canvas)

Dryad Ltd, Northgates, Leicester (Packets of coloured card, inexpensive canvas, tapestry wools and other kinds of embroidery threads)

John Lewis and Co. Ltd, Oxford Street, London W1 (Cushion pads)

List of suppliers (USA)

Supplies required for canvas embroidery may be purchased at the needle-work counter of most department stores, or at your local needlework shop. Or you may order by mail from the following sources, all of which carry a complete line of embroidery supplies, including embroidery frames, linen embroidery and rug canvas, crewel, tapestry, and carpet yarns, and all kinds of embroidery threads and sundries. Matting and framing supplies may be purchased at any art supply store.

Herrschners Needlecrafts, 72 E. Randolph St, Chicago, Ill. 60601

LeeWards, Elgin, Ill. 60120

LeJeune, Inc., 1098 W. Evelyn Ave., Sunnydale, Cal. 94086

Merribee Co., Box 9680, Fort Worth, Tex. 76107

Needlecraft House, West Townsend, Mass. 01474

The Stitchery, Wellesley, Mass. 02181

Erica Wilson, 40 East End Avenue, New York, N.Y. 10028

For additional information and suppliers, write to: Needlecraft Dept., McCall Pattern Co., 230 Park Ave., New York, N.Y. 10017

For further reading

Blackwork Embroidery by Elisabeth Geddes and Moyra McNeill; Mills and Boon, London 1965; Branford, Newton Centre, Mass. 1965

Canvas Embroidery by Diana Springall; Batsford, London 1969

Canvas Work: The Embroiderers' Guild, London

Canvas Work by M. A. Gibbon; Bell, London 1965; Branford, Newton Centre, Mass.

Canvas Work and Design by Jennifer Gray; Batsford, London 1960

Contemporary Embroidery Design by Joan Nicholson; Batsford, London 1954

Dictionary of Embroidery Stitches by Mary Thomas; Hodder and Stoughton, London; Toggitt, New York

Embroidery Stitches (*Needlework Stitches* US) by Barbara Snook; Batsford, London; Crown, New York

Ideas for Canvas Embroidery by Mary Rhodes; Batsford, London 1970

Inspiration for Embroidery by Constance Howard; Batsford, London 1966; Branford, Newton Centre, Mass. 1967

Stitchery for Children by Jacqueline Enthoven; Reinhold, New York 1968

The Stitches of Creative Embroidery by Jacqueline Enthoven; Reinhold, New York 1964

Index